Listen to The Voice Within

A Spiritual Journey

Rehel Anderson

ISBN 978-1-7366269-1-7

Dedication

This book is dedicated to everyone who is
seeking their spiritual path.

Table of Contents

Introduction

Rehel Anderson

I am a Spiritual Teacher and Author. My books aim to provide ways to enlighten the seeker and to attain their spiritual awakening through creativity, challenges, prayer, compassion and love. Challenges are our best teachers to help us grow more rapidly on our 'spiritual journey'.

With the many different careers or jobs in my life it gave me experiences that many would not be able to accomplish. I worked in fields planting vegetables, cleaning motels, a waitress, office work, secretary, TV model, owner of companies, speaker for Citizens Against Crime, held several offices in different organizations, and was in the movie industry 15 years before I retired.

In the movie industry I worked with the locations department, was an assistant to actors, directors, producers, a double for Kim DeLaney and Shirley Knight. I joined the Teamster's Union and carried a class A Commercial Driver license. I became a light stunt car driver.

Even though working in the movie industry was fun, it was some of the hardest times in my life.... but I loved it!

No matter what my current career was, I had the other side of me which was my spirituality. I called it my 'duality' life. I had all the questions everyone has in seeking a higher spiritual truth.

I developed my spiritual gifts and became a spiritual medium/channel/healer. I had a spiritual group which met twice a week for four years and met some of the most fascinating people within the spiritual community. Olaf Jonnson, who at the time was the most tested psychics in the world became one of my mentors. He worked with our government and Edgar Mitchell when they sent Mitchell to the moon. I met Dr. Leo Sprinkle from the University of Wyoming, Whitley Strieber, Stanton Friedman, and Brad Steiger, who were all tops in their field of UFO's, and there were many, many more.

I also walked away from my spirituality for several years. But, the one thing I had possessed was the 'knowingness' that I was not alone and could access my spirituality again when I was ready. I got back into my spirituality and awareness at the urging of so many friends when I was called upon to help in different scenarios. I am so glad that I did, as life is more meaningful when you are connected to GOD, a Higher Power/Force, universe, spirits, angels, guides and more.

At a very young age I had a *'knowing'* of spirituality. However, back then it was not called spirituality. It was mostly referred to as your *'intuition'*. And, even farther back in time there was little talk of your psychic abilities, your intuition, or spirituality. But a lot has transpired in the last decades. Our spirituality and knowingness are transforming more and more every day. We are seekers of Truth, seekers of our Purpose, 'Why' we are here, and much more. We are all looking for the answers to our questions because we are yearning for more in our lives and only a connection to a higher power, higher consciousness or that unseen force can supply. So, how do we go about that?

In these pages I will share with you some of my experiences of what can happen when you **Listen to the Voice Within** or what can happen when you don't **Listen to the Voice Within.**

It is my pleasure to share some of my knowledge with you. I hope that you find this information easy to read and understand.

Chapter 1

Our Physical Senses

We have five very important senses which are the sense of sight, smell, touch, taste, and sound. We also have our mind and intellect which contribute to our senses, and we have a sixth sense. Our sixth sense is very important to our spirituality. What is our sixth sense?

It is the ability to perceive the unseen world, angels, spirits, guides, and heaven. With our sixth sense we can develop ESP (extrasensory perception), clairvoyance, and premonition. We perceive the unseen world through our five senses, the mind, and our intellect, which is important to connect with the unseen world. We can develop or activate our sixth sense, and when we do, we will experience the unseen world, it is a *'spiritual experience'* like no other.

The unseen world or the Universal Mind is all around us and even though we cannot perceive it, it impacts our lives every day. In order to tune into this world, we need to learn how to connect to that world. As our spiritual level grows or our spirituality increases, it opens up to higher realms of connection.

The more we open up to the Universal Mind or the unseen world, with dedication and practice, you will hear that Voice Within.

There are many ways the *Voice* is speaking to you. It does not mean you always '*hear*' a voice. There are many ways '*how*' the voice speaks to you. It speaks to you in (gut) feelings, comments heard, seeing, noticing signs, an awareness, a knowingness of a situation, a thought that is not yours, and you wonder, is it your thought or is it the '*thought*' talking to me. You will know the difference with dedication and practice.

The more spiritually evolved you become you are able to differentiate whether it is your knowledge or the knowledge received from the Universal Mind or the Spirit World.

We have other aspects that influence our spiritual growth. Each individual possesses three important physical characteristics. They are visual, auditory and kinesthetic. Each individual is usually more prominent in one category than the other, but it is best to learn or have a balance in all three.

A **Visual** individual's learning style is *"Show me and I'll understand"*. They are cognizant or aware of their surroundings. They learn by being '*shown*' how to do something. They are more apt to '*see*' the coincidences that occur in their lives. They like to *see* what is going on. They are good in meditation when the unseen world *shows* them a vision, picture, words, or things.

Example: A visual person goes to buy clothes. They pick the item up, look at it, put it on, look in the mirror and *see* what they look like in the garment. They like to *see* it on them before they purchase the item.

Auditory individuals like to *'listen'*. They learn more from lectures, better than the visual or kinesthetic person. They learn best when being *'told'* how and what to do. They tend to read more, and listen to music. In meditation they are more apt to *'hear'* a message first. Sometimes, depending on the personality, they can be withdrawn or spend time alone. Many writers are strong in the auditory category.

Example: An auditory person goes to buy clothes. They look at it and *analyze* the item. They think about it several times before they try it on and then decide to purchase the item.

Kinesthetic individuals are the 'touchy, feely, and movement people. They like to touch everything. They like activities that move, such as sports, dance or cook. They learn best when the approach is with *'hands-on'*. In meditation they are more apt *to 'feel'* what is being received from the spirit world rather than seeing or hearing it. A kinesthetic person's second trait becomes visual before they are auditory.

Example: A kinesthetic person goes to buy clothes. They pick the item up and they *feel* the fabric. If they like how it *feels,* they try it on and as they look in the mirror, they rub and *feel* the fabric against their body. Depending on how it *feels* to them, they decide to purchase the item.

These three aspects are important in your development as your spirituality grows. These aspects are connected with the abilities of Clairsentience, Clairvoyance and Clairaudience.

What do these three aspects mean?

Clairsentient: clear *'sensing'* – the ability to *sense* smells projected by the spirit world, particularly smells associated with passed loved ones. It is the ability to send or receive information in an energy form that doesn't arrive as sight or hearing. It comes as a *'knowing'*. You simply *'know'* something. Everybody has the ability to be clairsentient. This is where you know of a phone call before the phone rings, or someone is thinking about you, or the sudden awareness you need to call someone or an awareness that changes are coming to you, all out of nowhere. Ask the spirit world to help you and to deliver the 'knowingness" so clearly that you will understand.

Clairvoyance: clear *'vision'* – This is the ability of *precognition* which is *seeing* future events. *Retro-cognition* is *seeing* past events. Clairvoyance is the ability to *see* an oncoming event in a picture. The picture is often a scene within. It isn't just a scene with the eyes; it's a scene behind the eyes, a scene in the heart that runs through you. Sometimes you *receive* *'flashes'* that give you clues of coming events. Maybe you will see white pin lights that appear to you and when you turn, they will be gone, or you will even see an actual light. You can see a cloud like mist, which could be spirit, or an entity from the unseen worlds.

Clairaudient: clear *'hearing'* – This is the ability to *hear* voices, or you might just have mental words appear in your head, much as they do when you are thinking. Often you have a *sound* that is muffled, sometimes in a distance, or often a *voice* in your head, or even *hearing* your name called.

These abilities come into play when you begin communicating with Spirit, and they become stronger the more you grow in your levels of spirituality. The spirit will develop a language with you so you will understand what is being communicated. They will also add clairsentient abilities to the clairaudient gift to help you get a much better picture of what is being related to you.

Chapter 2

Meditation Types

The most important way to connect to the Universal World, angels, and guides is to meditate. There are many ways to meditate. Search different ways to meditate so you can determine the meditation that resonates with you. There is no right or wrong way to meditate. I will share what works for me and some suggestions you might want to follow. But meditation is the key.

The four types of meditative states are:

Beta – normal wakefulness

Alpha – meditative state

Theta – deep meditation and learning

Delta – deep sleep

When you experiment and find what works for you, your *intention* is to sit silently and attune to a Higher Consciousness, that unseen world. Slow down your racing thoughts enough so you can hear the *voice* of *spirit*. Ask your chatter to step aside. Keep your mind blank so you can hear that *thought, feeling, or voice* that wants to come through to you from spirit. Your *intention* is to clear your mind in order to receive those spiritual messages.

You will always be guided. Your *intention* is to bring spirit to the forefront to feel peace, love and receive guidance. The stronger your *intention*, the easier it becomes when communicating with spirit. Spirit will never tell you anything bad, they will never tell you anything wrong, they will simply present themselves as love and light, and are eager to be of assistance.

When you meditate, find a place and time you are alone, quiet and uninterrupted. Find a comfortable position for you, preferably not lying down. If you are a beginner, it is best to sit with your feet on the floor/ground. It is not necessary to sit in a lotus position.

If I want to meditate to just become relaxed and peaceful, I will listen to soft and soothing music. This is the Alpha state of meditation. However, in deep meditation, the Theta state, I will not use music as it can deter or filter the voice within. At times I like to listen to a guided meditation (Alpha), which brings another type of experience during meditation. Some guided meditations have a purpose. For instance, if you want to lose weight, that guided mediation will support you in your goal to lose weight. That type of meditation helps your mind to attune to suggestions and prompting of the intent.

I use the different types of meditation, depending on what my *intention* is or what I am *asking* for. If I want to connect to the highest spiritual guidance, which is in Theta meditation, this is how I begin. I prefer night time when I am ready to go bed.

I place myself on my bed in a sitting up position with my legs stretched out with a small pillow under my knees to relieve any stress or tension. I make sure I am comfortable, not too cold or too hot. I have a small dim light to the side of the bed. When I settle down, I take several deep breaths, relax, and begin saying a prayer. I like to say 'Our Father". But you can use any prayer you are comfortable with. Each time, I say a prayer with all of the different meditations I use.

A prayer is protection. A prayer is talking to GOD. Meditation is GOD talking to you through and with the Spirit World. That's the importance of meditation. You connect with a higher power.

When I have settled down, I focus my attention on different parts of my body. I repeat the same statement when I focus on the body part I want to relax. I start at the top of my head and say to myself, "I relax my head, then I begin moving down the body saying, I relax my forehead, I relax my cheeks, I relax my jaw, I relax all the way down to the tip of my toes. I take a few deep breaths and continue. I relax my throat, I relax my shoulders, I relax my arms, I relax my chest, I relax all the way down to the tip of my toes. I take another couple of deep breaths and continue. I relax my stomach, I relax my hips, I relax my thighs; I relax all the way down to the tip of my toes. I take more deep breaths. I relax my knees, I relax my calves, I relax my ankles; I relax all the way down to the tip of my toes. At this point, I do feel that I am 'within' my physical body, but I do not focus on the physical body after that.

This type of meditation puts you in a slight hypnotic state where you are able to reach a Theta state of awareness.

In this very relaxed state of being, I sit quietly and *listen*. I allow my mind to become blank. It is then that I can begin to receive messages, thoughts, ideas, or insights. I am able to connect with a higher consciousness and the unseen world. When I finish this type of meditation, I love to roll over in bed, fall asleep, and many times messages come in my dreams, which is the deep state of Delta.

Premonitions can come in your dreams. So, pay attention. I find it helpful to write down your dreams as soon as you wake up. Keep a journal of your night time dreams and the messages you receive during the day or while in meditation.

In this state of Theta meditation, you can hear *'the voice'* within. And, as I stated before, it is not always audible to the ears. You will *know* or *sense* the information that is given to you. This is being *clairsentient.*

I must remind you it takes time, dedication and practice to reach higher spiritual levels. With practice you develop all of your sixth sense possibilities.

It depends on my intention, but I always start each meditation the same way by saying a prayer.

I mentioned I had different ways to meditate. Some simpler meditation is Beta. I use it while I am cleaning house, working in the yard, driving, or just in a day-dream state. I also call it, going *within or into my inner-world,* to talk to spirit, angels or guides. I *ask* them for help when I've lost an item, when I need something or just *asking* what can I do in any given situation. I *ask* for help in anything that I am trying to figure out. They are there to answer your questions, so don't be afraid to ask!

Keep a dialogue with spirit as if you are speaking to a friend. Spirit hears you.

What does *'going within'* mean?

It does not mean escaping, hiding, or retreating.

Some people think this means going within the body, to the center of our physical body and to pay attention. There is no need to focus on the body as it limits our consciousness (unless you are focusing on the parts of your body to go deeper into Theta mediation as I do). Let the physical body go. Don't focus on the body after you reach a deep relaxation point.

'Going *Within*' means going within states of consciousness, where you reach the 'real you'... the 'I AM' of one self.

With deep meditation you can open yourself up to higher levels of creativity, insight, inspiration, guidance, dreams, and wisdom.

When you use the different types of meditation the answers are available, but they may or may not come to you right away. But they will always come when you *ask with intent*, and have *faith* your questions are heard. Not always will you *'hear'* the answers or have a *'thought'* that gives you the answer. You may receive your answers by a coincidence, noticing things, something catches your attention, or you heard someone's comments, and there you find your answers. This is where all of your sixth senses come into play.

Don't try to make it happen, but allow it to happen. Surrender to the universe and have *faith*. Our intent is to become aware and *know* the voice within.

You may find another way to meditate which is best for you. Be diligent, dedicated and practice to attune to your sixth sense and connect with that voice of the unseen world.

When you master your meditation, you are taking the conscious mind to a higher level where it connects and accesses limitless possibilities. You connect to the Super-Conscious, the Universal Mind, Source, a higher power, guardian angels, and guides, all from the unseen world.

When you focus on the material world, it's easy to rely on the five physical senses for guidance, and this can lead you astray. Your intuition is your most reliable source. Your higher self and intuition will guide you. And, through meditation you can connect with all of

your helpers.

By meditating you will achieve a different state of consciousness than your normal waking state. When you connect with the Super conscious, it is all awareness and all knowing. You are tapping into Source and the unseen world.

Chapter 3
Spiritual Levels

There are many stages of awareness as you grow in your spirituality. We are all different and we will have different experiences. You cannot compare yourself to another person's experience or spiritual growth.

As you gain greater levels of spirituality, many gifts will be presented to you. And, you will *know* what these gifts are. Are they the gifts of clairsentience, clairvoyance, or clairaudience? Are you a medium, a channel, or a healer?

With the multitude of spiritual individuals that have become known in the last few decades, you will notice some are mediums, channels, healers, and teachers of many subjects pertaining to a spiritual path that we are seeking. Each one has a different style and yet have similar messages they are sharing from the higher power/higher force, and the unseen world.

If you notice the differences of spiritual gifts, some might only have one special gift while others possess several gifts. If you know of John Edward, his gift is to communicate with our loved ones from the other side. The same goes for the 'Long Island Medium'. Edgar Cayce was a healer who connected with the higher powers in order to heal while he was in a trance state. Esther Hicks is a wonderful channel that channels an entity called 'Abraham'. Neil Donald Walsh received messages from GOD whereby he wrote the book 'Conversations with God'.

Just look at the some of the prominent figures in the spiritual world like Wayne Dyer, Marianne Williamson, Deepak Chopra, Louise Hay and many more. All of these individuals have connected to God, Universal Mind, a higher force, and higher power.

As our spirituality is evolving and we have raised our energies and insights to a higher dimension, we are ascending in our consciousness and energies that helps the planet and others that are seekers.

Be patient while seeking what is the *truth* for you. Your dedication and connection to the higher power will bring excitement as you move from one stage to another. And, you do go from one stage of enlightenment to another on your journey of spirituality.

Chapter 4

Intuition

When I was very young and before I started on my spiritual path, I always had a *'knowing'*. My *intuition* was very strong. Intuitively I would know things before they happened. I knew if someone liked or disliked me. I knew if I pictured something in my mind strong enough it would happen almost identical as I had imagined. I even had the *'voice within'* before I knew anything about what the voice within was. I was gifted with clairsentience and clairvoyance, but I didn't know that. I thought everyone 'knew' what I knew and it was natural for everyone.

One day while at home I received a strong *intuition/premonition* that I was to gather my sons and immediately go see my grandmother as it would be the last time. I questioned it, but did exactly as the intuition/voice had told me. Of course, when I arrived at Grandma's house, she thought it a little odd that I was there on that particular day. I merely said that I wanted to see her. I was moving to Las Vegas soon and that was a good answer to give her. We did move to

Las Vegas and a week after moving there, I received the call that Grandma had passed away.

Not long after that my intuition gave me a *'feeling'* that I would be losing my dear Mother. Yes, that happened just as I had *felt*.

When you have the voice within, thoughts, feelings, or intuition, there is always a way that will confirm your insights. You realize the confirmation comes from somewhere and is not of your making.

We need confirmation to assure us we are on the right path. We will know it is not our thoughts or imagination, or our knowledge, but has come from the voice within. It is being received from the unseen world, our higher consciousness and more.

I had several insights and messages long before I made the decision to seek out my spiritual path. I thought everyone possessed this ability, and never knew it is a gift that was given me... probably from birth. But, all of us have intuition and it is up to us to learn how to increase its strength and how to pay attention to it.

When I started my spiritual journey, I started with meditation. I practiced meditation every night for one to two hours for months. I found that I was developing a cough while I was in this deep meditative state.

I was also seeking out spiritual groups and was fortunate enough to meet a 'card reader' named Tom Hart. He gave readings to people in many places around the world. He also had a spiritual group and invited me to attend. During one of our sessions, I could not stop coughing. Tom asked if this happened to me often or just when I attended his circle. I did not cough only when I was in meditation.

At that time, Tom talked me into a meditative state and there the cough turned into talking and I was giving messages from the other side. Wow, what a new step into my search on my spiritual path.

Tom became my mentor and we held our spiritual circle for several years, whereby I was able to grow rapidly in the levels of spirituality. We always started each circle with prayer and meditation, and we were open to whatever the universe wanted to share with us.

My experience while learning to meditate in our circle was that I did not *hear* the *'voice within'* at first. I am a visual person and I was *shown* (in my mind) a small TV with a ticker tape running at the bottom of the screen. As I watched the ticker tape, I began to read what was running across the screen. I knew what I was reading was not me, my thought, or my knowledge. I was connecting to Source, that higher power. This type of messaging continued for some time. As I looked and read the ticker tape messages, I began to read it out loud. A 'voice' of an *entity* was using my voice to deliver the messages. It was then I realized I had become a spiritual medium/channel.

I had grown rapidly and encountered tremendous spiritual experiences. I was able to give individual readings, communication from loved ones who had passed, healings, and was receiving information regarding our planet. Some were warnings and some were impressive insights and events that would occur in the future.

Chapter 5

Life Path

When you are on your own spiritual journey, be open to what the higher power has in store for you.

I say we have a 'blueprint' in heaven of our destiny. None of us always follow what is to be our destiny, but taking the journey on our life path to spirituality brings us closer to that destiny.

I define our 'Life Path' like this: We start our lives at point A and our *life path* is going to take us to point Z. As we travel along our path from point A, we journey to about point D and we decide to take a detour. By a detour I mean that we have made a decision to change our life or circumstances that may or may not be beneficial to us. And, many times we don't know it is not to our highest value. But God gave us free will to do whatever we choose to do. Our decision took us off our life path and away from reaching our destiny for a time being. When we left point D, we go along on our detour for a while, then an event or circumstance goes upside down or very wrong. We become unhappy, unsettled and life is not working out so well.

While we made those choices with our free will, Spirit has stood by, watched us, and allowed us to make our mistakes, encounter our challenges, but it is now time to get back on our life path to reach our destiny. Spirit comes along with a 'nudging force' and brings us back to point E to continue on our path. However, not all was lost. The challenges you encountered while on the detour were lessons that you were to learn from, and to help you grow in wisdom. You will do this many times on your *life path* to reach your destiny. You might take another detour at point L, another at point P, and the detours continue. Some detours may be shorter than others. You may also stay on the path to destiny longer than other times. It depends on your thinking, your desires and your free choices that you decide to make along your path. All of this is your life experiences, the good, the bad, and the ugly

Chapter 6

Meditation

There are so many benefits to meditation. Meditation is not just to communicate with the other realms of consciousness. It also helps us in our physical/material world. Regular meditation can resolve many of our problems at its core.

Meditation is *medication* and you have unlimited refills so why not have a meditation *habit*. Don't rely on pills to relieve problems with your mind or your physical body. You can eliminate so many causes or symptoms through meditation.

Meditation will give benefits for a healthier mind and body, and most of all, you will connect to the real you... the 'I AM'.

Meditation opens the doorway to the higher power of the universe, and the unseen spirit world.

What a gift we can give ourselves, both physical and mental, but most of all for our spiritual growth.

In an earlier chapter I explained the four types of meditation, Beta, Alpha, Theta, and Delta. Once you have progressed in your meditations, it is always a good practice to mediate in all four categories as it helps you attune to the unseen world and you will be able to hear the voice within so much faster and easier. That voice within becomes your friend. I never feel alone any more.... my friend is always there, and your friend will give you the answers you are asking for too. You are never alone!

Here are some examples of different states of meditation. I drove down a freeway in my normal wakeful state, which is the Beta state. While I was driving, I had some concerns, and said (in my head) "I don't know where to go or what to do". Then waited for an answer.

Here was my answer and my conversation with the voice within: "Go to the Anne Ree Colton Foundation". I said, "I don't know where that is" with intentions not to do it. Then the voice within immediately said, "What else do you have to do"? That was all the voice within said. When given instructions, most of the time I will take immediate action. I searched for the Anne Ree Colton Foundation and within one hour I located the Foundation only six blocks from where I was staying. Once I had gone to the Foundation wonderful things began to change in my life for the better. So, it is best to listen and take the instructions or guidance the unseen world is giving you. It is always better than your own choices.

While in an Alpha meditative state I asked what I should do for my health as I was having several issues which the doctors could not determine. Immediately I was given several things to do in order to correct those health concerns. Every time I complied to those instructions it was always for the better.

As a medium/channel I will go into the Theta deep meditation. In this state I receive many messages regarding our universe, planet, politics, and more, which I keep a record of as I always like to confirm what has been told to me.

Also, in the Beta state which I do most of the time now, I get silly and we have fun like it is a game. One time I was not satisfied after eating and nothing appealed to me. I asked if there was anything that would stop this feeling of wanting more and not being satisfied. What a laugh I got… "Eat bread and gravy". Well, I fixed bread and gravy, and I had no more feelings of wanting anything else. I was totally satisfied.

Chapter 7

I AM

What does the 'I AM' mean?

In the Bible it tells of Moses when he was on the mountain speaking with God. When Moses encountered God, Moses asked God "What is your name?" and God replied, "I AM THAT I AM".

God is Source, God is love; God is ALL. The Bible tells us that we are made in God's image. So, if we are made in His image, we *are* love, pure love, and all that is, is who *we* are. It is where our highest self begins to recognize our own Divinity and God.

When we recognize we are God or the I Am, we must be aware of the importance of I AM. Whenever we say out loud, *I AM*, it can enlighten us or hinder us, depending on what way we say it.

If we have positive thoughts and a positive attitude our words are powerful. When you say "I am happy, I am kind, I am grateful, I am generous, I am love, I am wealth, I am spirit, I am abundance, I am thankful, I am open minded, I am determined, I am confident, I am successful, I am truth, I am good, I am kind, I am strength, I am energy," and much more, it is then we are *with* God, and we *are* perfect and unlimited!

I AM is your pure being, true nature, power source and no one else is the God in you. When you say I AM one with God, you are improving your life. And, whatever you *attach* to I AM, that you become.

You must be careful how you use I AM when speaking. When you are having negative thoughts or a negative attitude and you say "I am stupid, I am not beautiful, I am sick, I am lonely, I am scared, I am worried, I am useless, I am not deserving, I am weak, I am poor, I am unable, I can't, I won't, I don't have, etc., *it is stopping the great presence of God within you.* Turn your statements around and say "I am smart, I am pretty/handsome, I am in perfect health, I am loved, I am not afraid, I am not worried, I am useful, I am deserving, I am strong, I am abundant, I am capable, I can, I will, I do have, etc.

When you say statements of a negative nature, you are disgracing God. He is our Creator. Do not demean Him in anyway, because God is not any of these negative things. He is pure Love and Light. Your negative thoughts are only in your own mind and your own thoughts. Become God like. Live in His image. And, we can do that when we are seeking our spiritual path.

There are times you may feel all of these negative things, but, change your language and when you change the *I Am* words to a positive, it changes the energy and you become that which you speak.

When you live in the light and connect to Source, you begin to attract what you desire and the possibilities are unlimited.

Whenever I am asked "how are you today", I like to say "I am great, how are you." I know the more I say that I am great, the 'greater' I become. And, that is what all of us want for ourselves, is it not?

Chapter 8

How to Ask the Spirit World

When you have found *your* Voice Within and you know how to connect with Source or the higher power, it is time to understand how best to use it.

It is your job to connect with spirit, not the other way around. Get past your humanness and rid yourselves of the mind chatter so you can elevate your energies. When you do, spirit realigns to your energy/vibration pattern and attunes to you.

Spirit is ever present waiting to give you instructions, inspirations, and to be of service to you. All you have to do is ask. Remember, in the Bible is states *"Ask and it shall be given."* It does not say *'want'* and it shall be given. If you say to spirit "I want a new car". Well, spirit gives you the *'wanting'* of the new car, not the new car.

There is another language that moves spirit to give you what you are asking for. I like to use both statements:

1. I, (state your name) ASK for ....

It is very important to be specific what you are asking for:

Example: I, (state your name) ask for a new 2021 Black Mercedes automobile with four doors, sun roof, radio, etc. See what I mean by specific? And, you can elaborate more with specifics so it is very clear to spirit what they are to provide for you.

2. I (state your name) would like to **have** the experience of a new relationship. I would like him/her to be of good character, approximately my age, same spiritual values, likes to travel, likes to dance, etc. And, again be very specific in the *experience* you are asking for. When you feel you have *asked* for or like *to have* the *experience* of, in specific details to spirit, close your statement by saying to the universe/spirits *"that it be done in the perfect way"*. Spirit wants to provide you with your desires when you have a sincere *intention* and *belief* it will be received.

   Note: If you are not comfortable in number two when I say "I would like to "have", you can also say "I *ask* for the *experience* of............. The key words are ASK and HAVE. I did not say 'want'.

Many times, when we ask our spirits or guides, we simply say "I'd like a new car". Well, you will get a new car, but was it the one you would like to have?   Spirit gave you what was *available*. You must put your request in specifics so spirit *knows* your true desire.   Spirit is not going to read your mind.

Example: You go into Starbucks. You say to the clerk you would like a Grande Coffee.   The clerk gives you a Grande cup of coffee.   However, you neglected to say, "I would like a Grande Cafe Mocha, with whipped cream, a cherry on top and could you please sprinkle some cinnamon on the top, please"? That's a big difference, and by being specific, the clerk can make your Grande coffee exactly as you asked.   She couldn't read your mind when you only asked for a Grande Coffee.

How many times have we heard, "I just want a man/woman in my life"?   Spirit did comply and got the first man/woman to your liking or is available, and when the relationship becomes intolerable and you want to break up or get a divorce, you wonder why.   Spirit fulfilled your request the best way spirit knew how because you were not specific in what you would really like to experience in this relationship.   You asked for a man/woman, you got the easiest and most available at the time.   Remember, be careful what you ask for, you might get it!

This is my story of what happened when I was not specific in what I was asking the universe for. I asked for a new job, a new house with 3 bedrooms, 2 baths and a swimming pool, a new boyfriend and a new Lincoln. Within thirty days I received a new job, the new house and a man named 'Lincoln', because I did not specify the Lincoln was an automobile! Later I did receive the Lincoln automobile. Lessoned learned.

Another very important thing to remember when connecting or communicating with the universe or spirit world, don't tell the universe what you *don't* want. Always make it a positive intention and always be *grateful* and *thank* them for all the assistance they give you.

When spirit provides you with all that you ask for, it may not be when or how you think it is to come to you. There is a great *'timing'* in the universe, so don't expect it your way. It is important for you not to doubt or give up. You are to *believe* that spirit will provide what you are anticipating.

If you are asking for a relationship, it may be two or three years in the future because the other special person is not quite finished with circumstances or is not ready at the same time, or you may not quite be ready for this relationship. Spirit will present it in the *perfect way* and in the *perfect timing* for you and the person involved.

Turn loose of control on an issue when you are asking for something. With Universal love and intention there are no limitations. You only limit yourself, not spirit. Guidance is endless and it opens doors to all possibilities.

When you ask in prayer for everything you would like to have in your life, do not keep repeating this same prayer as it drives spirit a little bonkers and most importantly it relates as 'I don't deserve it, and I don't trust you'. *Ask* in prayer, *believe it* and *expect* it to come your way in the *perfect timing, in the perfect way.*

Chapter 9

Spirit Instructions & Guidance

Now that we have learned *how* to ask the universe/higher power for what we would like in our life, it is time to learn how to *listen* when the unseen world is talking to you with *instructions* and *guidance* to help further your life path in a positive way to reach your destiny. It is also 'their' way of asking you to comply... for your benefit.

It is so important to understand what the spirit world is *instructing* and *guiding* you to do. The higher power always directs you in a positive and productive way to assist you on your life path. So, how could you go wrong?

I know how very important it is to comply with the higher power guidance, as I created some difficult times for myself when I did not listen to the higher power.

I was stubborn and thought it best to use my *free will* instead of listening and doing as I was being directed from the spirit world. I was using my five senses and letting my ego get in the way.

Back in the late '80's I had moved to Reno, Nevada. One day as my mind was chattering and wondering what I should do for the day, the silent *voice*, *thought*, and a moving *picture* came strong into my head.

There are several ways the spirit world attempts to get your attention.

I was being *told* and *shown* that I was to go to the nearest 7-11 store, buy some snacks, and drive to Truckee, California to buy a lotto ticket with these numbers at a certain 7-11 store. I started to argue with spirit and said that I didn't drive that far by myself and why would I want to do that???

I tried to dismiss this very powerful instruction, but it repeated itself three more times so strong that I finally relented.

I drove to the nearest 7-11 store, bought several snacks to eat on the way to Truckee and had the intention of doing as I was instructed. I kept seeing in my head *where* I was to go, and when I was coming to an exit that would take me into Truckee, I heard a loud *voice* that shouted "take this exit"!

Well, my ego and stubborn self said "no, I'll take the next exit". As I took the next exit and came to a stop sign, the picture entered my head of the 7-11 where I was to purchase the lotto ticket, which would have taken me to the right and just a few blocks away. But again, I argued and decided I would do it my way... you know that *'free will'* that crept in. Instead of turning right as instructed, I turned left and drove to Squaw Valley instead of doing as spirit had instructed me. Surely, there would be another 7-11 store where I could purchase the lotto ticket I thought.

As soon I as I drove into Squaw Valley to my right, I saw a 7-11 store. I went straight away to get a lotto ticket and marked out the numbers that spirit asked me to play.

The lotto drawing was a very large one and there were many people standing in line to purchase their tickets. I stood in line with everyone and when I reached the clerk to purchase the lotto ticket, the machine would not take my ticket. The clerk tried several times, but it would not take my ticket. Several people kept saying "She has the winning ticket". And, each time the clerk attempted to put my ticket into the machine, it still would not take the ticket. The customers kept saying "She has the winning ticket". The clerk commented that was just my ticket and she had me rewrite that ticket 5 different times. The customers began to argue with the clerk saying "The machine takes everyone's ticket it just isn't taking hers".

It became quite a spectacle. At the last resort, the clerk finally called the manager. The manager opened the lotto machine and as she did, the containers of jerky and sausage that were in front of the machine fell down and the containers hit the top of my foot. Now, I was injured and the next half hour I spent filling out an accident report. I did not purchase my lotto ticket.

Oh, I was in pain and all I could think about was getting into the car and driving a couple of blocks to the Truckee River and to put my ever so swelling foot in the ice freezing water.

As I sat on the river bank, I did my best to talk to spirit.... But, nothing! I kept open and waited and still no message. It got so late that I knew it was time to return to Reno. As I drove down the mountain, I continued asking spirit, "What am I to do"?

Why was I asking? Spirit had already talked to me, gave me instructions and guidance! I did not do as I was asked, so why did I expect an answer?

Then spirit put me to a test. I heard, "Stop at McDonald's". I began to argue in my head again! Then I decided to pay attention. I asked "What do you want me to do"? Spirit said "Go to the restroom". So, I went to the restroom. As I was leaving McDonald's, I heard "Buy a hamburger".

I started to argue again saying, "I don't eat McDonald's hamburgers". Just stop it I thought.

At that point I thought I better do as I am told, so I bought a hamburger, got into my car and heard nothing more. I decided to drive to the first 7-11 store that I had been *shown* in my mind, and there I would purchase the lotto ticket.

As I drove into the parking lot I was in such pain with my injured foot, I sat there and sat there and decided I was in too much pain to try to walk into the store to purchase a lotto ticket. I put the car in gear and drove back to Reno.

When I arrived home, my only thought was to go upstairs to bed, prop up my foot and watch TV. Oh, what a day I had.

Later the news was coming on and I wanted to be sure I listened for the winning lotto numbers. Sure enough, the numbers I was to play were the winning numbers, and I had not played my ticket!!!!!! NO, no, no!!

This was one of the greatest lessons I had. And, this is what can happen when you *do not listen* to what spirit is guiding and instructing you to do.

I can only imagine how my life might have turned out had I listened to this very important message. And, what did spirit want me to accomplish with this amount of money? Millions!!

Spirit followed with this message, "you will not have this opportunity again".

Needless to say, this was not the only time I let my ego and free will come into play when I was being strongly instructed and guided by the higher power. Unfortunately, I did this more times than I would like to count.

I can only advise you, please do not do as I did for the consequences are great. And, sorry to say, I had more lessons and challenges than I wanted because I was stubborn, I let my ego get in the way, and I chose to utilize my free will.

The big lessons were to trust in spirit, leave the ego behind, not to be so stubborn, and not put such emphasis on free will, especially when spirit comes to you with such a gift to help improve your life. This is not always easy for anyone, and I was one of the most difficult students of the spirit world, don't you be as difficult. Please, pay attention and be open to the wonders that can be presented to you.

This obviously states I was not trusting in spirit and I let my humanness and five senses lead me astray, and I didn't take the opportunity to act on the wonderful instructions and guidance that I was being given to better my life.

The opposite happened when I *did listen* to instructions and guidance from the great beyond.

Many years ago, I was always seeking ways to heighten my spiritual journey. I found groups, books, conferences, lectures, etc. I wanted to attend a conference being held at the University of Wyoming in Laramie, Wyoming. I drove there alone around the 4th of July.

After I arrived, I was quite aware that I was starting to have car problems. Several men at the conference were kind enough to look at my car to see if they could help, but that wasn't the case. I took my car to different mechanics and dealerships and I was told each place was too busy to service my vehicle. I got very concerned as it was the 4th of July weekend and I knew I would be in trouble if I couldn't find a mechanic right away. I was getting worried and frustrated and didn't know what to do.

The next morning, I went back to the conference. I was still feeling very anxious inside when I *heard* the *voice within* and *saw* a picture.

The voice said, "Take your car on this road to the place we are showing you, and please go alone and tell no one."

We broke for lunch. I excused myself and drove on the road I had never driven on before, and was looking for the area that I had been shown. Finally, I spotted the area I was to go to, but I could not see a road or any way to get there. After doing the best I could, and still could not reach the area, I decided to turn around and go back to the conference. I didn't know what else to do. As I was driving back, out of the corner of my right eye, I caught a glimpse of a dirt road. Promptly the *voice* wanted me to take that road until I came to a plateau. There was nothing but sagebrush, gravel and weeds. Then the *voice* said, "Stop, get out of the car and walk in a circle and don't go near the green bush." As I looked around, I saw a small green bush not more than ten or twelve inches high. I walked in a circle around the green bush and I kept walking but I heard nothing. In my head I thought to myself, "if anyone sees me, they are going to think I'm stark raving crazy and I'm not too sure of it myself."

I walked for about twenty minutes. In the distance I saw a motorcycle coming in my direction and I became concerned for my safety. I was a female, alone, in the desert, and a long way from town. Instantly I heard, "Get in your car and leave". I immediately got in the car and drove back to Laramie as I was instructed. Then the *voice* said, "Stop at the Subway Sandwich shop, have a half tuna sandwich and a coke. Go back to the conference, and, oh, by the way, your car is fixed"!

Wow, I had my car fixed and lunch was ordered before I went back to the conference. How good was that??? And, the best was.... I never had a mechanical problem with my car before I sold it several years later.

Can you understand how wonderful it can be when you don't resist the instructions and guidance of the higher realms? My advice is to work with them, follow their instructions to the T if you can, but do the best you can as your life will be better for it.

There are different ways the spirit world is guiding you for your benefit. You must learn and pay attention and understand what and why the spirit world is directing you to do something.

Again, many years ago, a friend of mine wanted me to go out dancing with her. I loved to dance and it was a wonderful way to relax and unwind from my busy schedule. We were having a wonderful time and decided to sit at our table for a while since we had danced almost every dance.

She had become friendly with a man she had been dancing with. He said to me that his friend would be arriving shortly and perhaps I would like him. I instantly thought "oh no, this is not my type of guy", especially if the friend was anything like him. I wanted nothing to do with him. Shortly, in walked his friend. I took one look at him and instantly the *voice* said, "You will marry this man." I was almost shouting in my head, "no, no, no"! There was no attraction and the more I learned about him I could not figure out why the spirit world would have me marry this type of man.

To make a long story short, we were married a few months later. And, almost instantly after getting married I became quite ill. I had three tumors in my head that required surgery. I had lost most of my family and there was no one I could have turned to for help in my condition. I still had my father, but this was not a situation he could have handled. Spirit brought this man into my life to marry, to support and help me as I was headed for a difficult time.

I had two sons that appreciated and respected him. He was a great nurse and helped me in every way possible when I was unable to help myself. He was my support system for the four years it took to recover. When I fully recovered and was able to take care of myself and my children, our marriage dissolved as quickly as it had begun. I expressed it like 'poof', gone! It ended and there was no more to it.

I was so grateful to spirit for sending this man into my life and I *'knew'* what and why it was meant to be. Even though there was a shady side to his character, spirit knew how kind, supportive and helpful he would be to me and my sons to help me through this difficult time in my life. Thank you spirits!

As you can see, there are so many ways spirit instructs, guides, and assists; because there are so many times, we may not be able to help ourselves in some situations. Spirit will always give us the help when we need it, even though we aren't able to understand it at the time.

I have dozens of stories that I can relate to you that are wonderful, positive experiences, and I can also tell you many stories that were not so wonderful because I did not listen and did not do as I was instructed. However, not all was lost, as each challenge gave me lessons that I appreciated and I gained a lot of wisdom from each experience. Of course, not at the time it was happening! Hind sight is wonderful, isn't it?

I would like my experiences and words to impact you in some way that you do your best not to do what I did. Follow the Source, the higher power, spirits and angels, you will not be disappointed.

Chapter 10

Dialogue with Spirit

While you are on your spiritual path, you want to have the ability to *hear* and be able to communicate with spirit and the unseen world.

For many people on their spiritual path, when they receive answers, it may sound like their own conscious mind, and sometimes it is hard to tell the difference between the voice of spirit and your own conscious mind.

As I stated before, Spirit will never tell you anything bad, they will never tell you anything wrong, they simply present themselves as love and light, and are eager to assist.

You will be able to differentiate if the knowledge that is coming to you is from spirit or if it is your own knowledge. And, again, it takes diligence and dedication on your part while seeking a higher level of spirituality.

Your dedication becomes a habit. I like to make a habit of speaking to spirit when I first wake up in the morning. I express to spirit all the things I am *grateful* for. And, each day I like to pray to spirit saying, please help me to *hear* and *learn* what I am meant to learn today. Please make it very clear to me so I will understand. Help me block any negative thinking for this day. I am willing to serve, thank you spirit.

You can also ask spirit to remove any road blocks and obstacles for your highest good.

As you believe and have faith, you develop a quiet 'knowing' where you will feel motivated and excited to do more. You can feel your consciousness being changed. You can actually feel spirit working within you. You can also *feel* when you are off your spiritual path.

As you develop more habits, another good way to reach higher levels of ascension is to *journal*. A journal is a tool to release all that is built up in you, so you will be super open to receive more from Source.

Journaling is your own best psychologist. It releases worries, anxiety, hurt, grudges, resentment, and more. Journaling can also widen and expand your perspectives of your imagination and ideas you might have for the future. You gain more by writing it down. It will open new avenues for your personal and spiritual growth. Journaling helps you to resolve some of your life issues when you write it down. For instance, if you journal some situation that has hurt you, have a grudge, resentment, or worries, etc., by journaling your issue, and when you connect to those *feelings* related to the issue, it then releases the *issue* and the *feelings* from your body and your life. It is cleansing your spirit. You may not forget, but you will not be stuck in that issue you have written down in your journal. Typing it out on the computer is okay too. It works the same way because you are expressing it in your own words.

In my daily dialogue with spirit, I will say "YES YES, YES", to let them know I am willing to participate in life to reach my destiny, and that I will stay in divinity. In divinity we receive miracles and other wonders. The universe will create it and we must *know* we deserve it. Saying *yes* is allowing or making us move forward in a positive way. We are open to the wonders of the unseen world which will be presented to us.

The more we *know* that we deserve, it is easier to say "I am wealthy, I am abundant, I am happy, I am fulfilled, I have everything that I have imagined or visualized.

See the possibilities, isn't it wonderful?

Train your mind to imagine. Then, turn your imagination into visualization. We tend to limit our mind or our thinking in both categories.

There is a great way to expand your imagination. First, if money was no object, what would you have or what would you do?

Many people are limited by saying, "I'd buy a new home, a new car, go on vacation, buy some new clothes, help my family".

But what if you expanded your imagination to, I would own a private airplane, I would own a huge yacht, I would have every kind of vehicle I desired. I would travel any part of the world I wished to see. I could stay in the White House. I would own jewels and art of all kinds. I would have homes in several different countries. I would have a make-over by the tops in the field, and wear the best clothes. I would have staffs of employees to handle all legal and personal affairs. And, the list goes on and on. Can you see how you could play the game of imagination? Be audacious, and elaborate more and more every time you play the imagination game!

When you play the game of imagination, it opens up all possibilities for Source to know that which you *truly* desire. You are not limiting yourself. And, there are no rules that say, "You can't have it all". We limit ourselves, not the universe!

Your imagination is great. However, to make it come into reality you must use the art of visualization to turn the imagination into something that will then become real.

When you visualize anything, it is important to *see* it and to *feel* it. The *seeing it* and *feeling it* makes it real, while only the imagination is a thought and all thoughts turn into ideas and those ideas put into action while visualizing it, it then begins to create it in the material world.

Of course, just because we say it, doesn't mean we will get it. We must take into account the importance of what *YOU* would really like or desire for yourself. You may not want to have a private airplane or even like to travel. That is not the point. The point is to expand your mind so *you* can become limitless in the possibilities of what you are asking the universe for. Don't limit yourself.

Chapter 11

Conclusion

In searching for our spiritual path, we must learn how to reach our spirituality just like learning a new language or playing the piano. It takes time and it can be accomplished. You don't master it in a day. Learn the art of stillness, the art of giving, the art of kindness, and the art of compassion. Learn to *see* who you are and be able to access that part of you to understand and *know* you better. Learn to *give freely* in order to get back in return. Remember, what you give out, you get back. Live in divine thought and action.

When you are in complete stillness, you are hearing the "Voice Within". It is a wiser voice than your own. You have connected to Source!

Listen to the *Voice Within*. It will lead you to your purpose and guides you to your destiny. True happiness is *within*!

I hope this book has given you the tools to guide you and to help you develop the spirituality that you are seeking, and to guide you along your spiritual journey, as well as understand why it is important to do so.

I leave you with this prayer.

GOD, I ask You and the Spirit World to guide and transform my life today and every day.
Show me how I may serve.
Thank you, I am so grateful!

Thank you for taking the time to read my book. I pray it helps guide you on your spiritual journey.

Many blessings.

Rehel

Rehel Anderson's Books

W o W Woman of Wonder
A Spiritual Journey

A How to Guide
Listen to the Voice Within

www.ingramcontent.com/pod-product-compliance
Lightning Source LLC
Chambersburg PA
CBHW071736020426
42331CB00008B/2056